BMW

BMW

DON MORLEY & MICK WOOLLETT

Published in 1992 by Osprey Publishing
59 Grosvenor Street, London W1X 9DA

ISBN 1 85532 275 7

Page design Angela Posen
Printed in Hong Kong

Half-title page
*The 800 cc Touring 80/7 with wire wheels
and nosecone as standard*
Right
*One of the sweetest ever BMWs to ride,
the larger capacity R75/5 of the early
1970s*

For a catalogue of all books published by Osprey Automotive
please write to:
**The Marketing Department, Octopus Illustrated Books,
1st Floor, Michelin House, 81 Fulham Road, London SW3 6RB**

Contents

A flying start

If Germany had won World War 1 would there have been a BMW
motorcycle? Almost certainly not for it was only when the Treaty of Versailles,
imposed on Germany by the victorious Allies in 1919, forced the company to
stop aircraft engine production and diversify, that motorcycle production was
even considered.

Even then powered two-wheelers were far from their first choice.
Agricultural machinery, office equipment and furniture, tool boxes, braking
systems, a four-cylinder, eight-litre engine for possible marine, stationary and
truck application were all manufactured at the Munich factory before BMW
drifted into the motorcycle world.

The ancestry of BMW (the initials stand for *Bayerische Motoren Werke* –
Bavarian Motor Works) can be traced right back to Nikolaus August Otto the
German internal combustion engine pioneer who perfected the first four-
stroke engines in the mid 1880s. For it was his son Gustav who founded the
Gustav Otto Flugmaschinenfabrik in Munich in 1911 which amalgamated
with the Bayerische Flugzeugwerke (BFW) to form BMW in 1917. Chief
engine designer at BFW was Max Friz and the first BMW engine to go into
production was a six-cylinder overhead-camshaft unit which won acclaim –
notably from Manfred von Richthofen, the famous 'Red Baron', who was
Germany's top fighter pilot and already a world famous figure. He praised the
engine after tests and almost certainly used early production units in the
Albatros aircraft he flew when he scored the majority of his 83 'kills'.
However, he was not BMW powered when he was shot down and killed in
April 1918. On that fateful day he was flying a Fokker triplane with a rotary
Oberursel engine.

The fact that BMW were in the forefront of aero-engine design, despite a
late start compared to Mercedes, Daimler, Benz and Maybach, was again
proven when an Albatros single-seater, fitted with a BMW 111a 185 bhp
water-cooled, in-line, six-cylinder engine, reached the record altitude of 34,450
feet during German airforce tests in 1918.

Altitude performance continued to be something of an obsession with BMW
even after the end of the war and in the summer of 1919 a DFV biplane,
powered by an uprated BMW engine with a capacity of 19 litres and a power

*The English ABC exhaust over the inlet
valve opposed twin of 1913, one of BMW's
early role models*

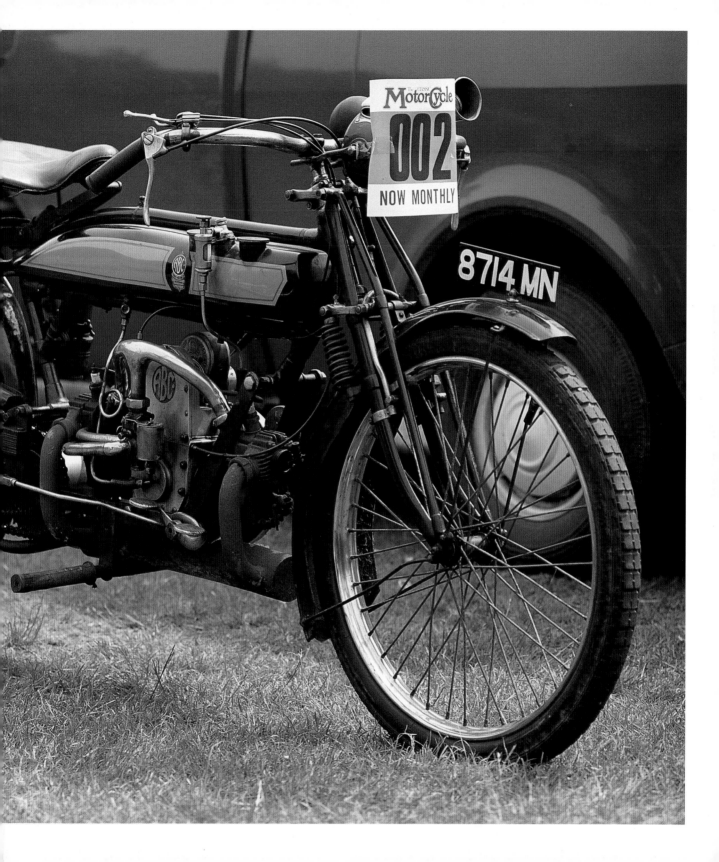

Above

Many thousands of 2¾ horsepower Douglas's (similar to this 1914 version) served on the Somme during the Great War

Opposite above

BMW's long serving roundel was designed after a rotating propeller

Opposite below

FN of Belgium even used shaft drive on their pre-1914 motorcycles

output of 250 bhp, carried pilot Franz Diemer to an official altitude record of just over 32,000 feet which was less than the wartime figure, but that had not been achieved under official scrutiny.

Such aerial activity was strictly forbidden under the terms of the Treaty of Versailles and the angered Allies promptly confiscated the engine and made it clear to BMW that from now on they were to concentrate on peaceful earth-bound projects. This accelerated the drift into new ventures and the first flirtation with a two-wheeler was to build and market a little single-cylinder lightweight powered by a 148 cc two-stroke engine designed by Curt Hanfland and built by Kurier. Named the Flink this was on sale from 1920 to 1922 but was not a success.

While the Flink was being produced BMW were working on their first flat-twin engine. This was based on the Douglas design used so successfully by both British and French despatch riders in the war. Captured models had obviously impressed the Germans and the Douglas was certainly ahead of the Continental designs of the time.

The new unit was code-named M2B15 and like the Douglas it was designed to be mounted fore-and-aft in the frame with chain drive to the gearbox. Bore and stroke were square at 68 × 68 mm to give a capacity of 494 cc. Power output of this side-valve engine was a lowly 6 bhp but it was a relatively neat package and was soon being bought by a number of small manufacturers to power their machines – notably Victoria, Corona, Heller, Scheid, Heninger, SMW and Bison.

This was the first motorcycle engine to bear the famous BMW initials and the quartered blue and white trade mark which was chosen to depict the spinning propeller of the aircraft engine. After selling the first engines to other companies to build into their own machines BMW decided to market a complete motorcycle in 1922. This was trade marked the Helios with the M2B15 engine installed in a frame built, but not designed, by BMW.

It proved a short-lived experiment. It was not a good machine and chief engine designer Max Friz was far from impressed. Although not a motorcyclist he could appreciate the faults of the Helios and assisted by Martin Stolle he set out to design the first complete BMW motorcycle – the R32.

To achieve better cooling he swung the engine through 90 degrees so that the two cylinders stuck out one on each side. Then to eliminate chains the separate gearbox was replaced by one which was in unit with the engine – bolted to the rear as in a car – and like a car the drive to this was via a large, single-plate clutch.

Drive to the rear wheel was by shaft. There was nothing revolutionary about these changes. Both had been tried and proven in previous designs, notably by ABC of England who marketed a horizontal transverse 398 cc twin in 1919 and by the Belgian FN company who pioneered shaft drive on motorcycles in 1904. But this was the first time they had been brought together in one design.

The engine retained the 68×68 mm bore and stroke of the earlier unit but the power had been raised to 8.5 bhp with maximum revs of 3300. This gave a top speed of around 55 mph but more importantly a cruising speed of 40 mph.

But the R32 was not simply a new engine, the frame had received a lot of attention. The flimsy tube layouts into which the M2B15 had often been installed was replaced by a sturdy, duplex layout in which twin tubes ran down from the steering head, under the engine and back to support the rear wheel before curving up and over the fuel tank to the steering head. This made for a rather heavy but very sturdy layout, the complete machine weighing 264 lb.

The front fork, too, was new. The wheel was carried on short trailing arms with the movement controlled by rods coupled to a leaf spring which jutted out just above the front mudguard. Only in the braking department did Friz and Stolle not take advantage of the latest technology – they stuck to an already out-dated v-block on dummy belt rim at the back and, initially, no brake at all at the front although a small drum brake was fitted to the R32 series 2 in 1924.

Certainly the first ever BMW was a sensation when it was launched at the Paris Show in 1923. In all 3090 R32s were built between that launch and 1926 when it was replaced. Not a staggering figure by today's standards but good for the early 1920s, for a high-priced luxury model. BMW were now in the motorcycle market and more models soon followed.

Racing and records

When the R32 was launched and the terms of the Treaty of Versailles were eased Max Friz returned to his first love, aero-engines. Stolle left BMW to join Victoria in Nuremberg and it was Rudolph Schleicher, a keen competition rider, who took over the reins as chief designer at BMW.

His first project was the second BMW motorcycle – the sporting R37. This retained the square 68 × 68 mm bore and stroke inherited from Douglas but the performance inhibiting side-valves were replaced by pushrod operated overhead valves. The valve gear was fully enclosed and the valves operated in light alloy cylinder heads bolted to barrels which were machined from solid billets of steel.

A selection of early race BMW or sports bikes on show at the Hockenheim GP Circuit Museum

The overhead valves, allied to a higher compression ratio literally doubled the power from 8.5 to over 16 bhp at 4000 rpm to give the 295 lb machine a top speed of around 70 mph. The prototype ran in 1924 when the factory supported rider Franz Bieber raced one to win the German road-racing championship, and in 1925 the R37 went on sale alongside the R32.

It was, however, an expensive prestige machine and only 152 models were built in two years – including ten special competition versions which were sold to selected road racers and trials riders. Riding a factory bike, designer Schleicher came to England in 1926 and won a gold medal in the International Six Days' Trial. This was the first time a German rider had won a 'gold' in an ISDT held in the UK and Professor A M Low, a well-known authority of the time and technical chief of the organizing British Auto-Cycle Union wrote: 'The most interesting machine of the whole meeting was undoubtedly the German BMW. A horizontally opposed two-cylinder engine

Above

A now exceedingly rare Ing Max Friz designed OHV 750 cc R63 of 1928, which incidentally was good for 65 mph uphill or down and cost just over £178 in the UK

Overleaf

The 482 cc side valve R52 of 1928 just oozed quality and compared to most bikes then on the market was years ahead of its time

Opposite and overleaf

When the Berlin Wall fell, Wallace Lambert brought this unrestored R52 back from behind the former Iron Curtain, and all it needed to comply with today's laws was a set of new tyres

which is mounted transversly in the frame – with completely enclosed valve gear, block construction and shaft drive. Even after the hardest days there wasn't a bit of oil to be seen anywhere, the machine was beautifully quiet and seemed to have an enormous power reserve. It is miles ahead of any British machine as far as design is concerned.'

On the home front the R37 won close to 100 road races in 1925 including the 500 cc class of the German Grand Prix though it is fair to say that at that time the 'German' was not a major international event. That same year BMW broadened their range by producing their first single-cylinder machine – the R39. This was a 247 cc machine with the single 'pot' rising vertically from the crankcase with the same 68 × 68 mm bore and stroke. The car type clutch, unit-construction, three-speed gearbox and shaft drive were retained.

The R39 was in fact half an R37 for the engine had pushrod operated overhead valves and produced 6 bhp at 4000 rpm – a high performance for a 250 cc machine in 1925. This gave the little BMW a top speed of around 60 mph and in tuned, racing trim it proved a formidable competition machine. Riding one of these Josef Stelzer won the quarter-litre class of the 1925 German road-racing championship.

By this time all three models had internal expanding drum front brakes and the old-style dummy belt rim rear brakes had been replaced by a transmission brake. This was heel operated and acting on a small disc situated on the drive shaft just behind the gearbox.

In 1926 the R42 was phased in to replace the R32. It is worth noting here that the model numbers jumped because certain numbers were allotted to prototype machines which never went into production – so out of the 11 spanned by the numbers R32 to R42 only four actually went on sale.

The new machine was essentially an up-dated R32. Detachable light alloy cylinder heads replaced the one-piece cast-iron cylinder and head of the original side-valve and power was up by some 50 per cent at 12 bhp at 3400 rpm. To make way for the drum front brake the speedometer drive had been moved from the hub to the gearbox. During a two-year production run 6502 machines were built.

For 1927 the overhead valve R39 was replaced by the R47 with power boosted by 2 bhp – from 16 to 18 bhp. Unlike the first sports model, of which only 152 were built, the R47 went into full production and during its two-year factory 'life' 1720 machines were sold.

In 1928 both models were up-dated. The R52 replaced the R42 and the R57 took the place of the R47. The engines were little changed but the gearboxes had been modified (though still hand-change without the option of foot operation which was becoming increasingly popular among British manufacturers), the exhaust pipes ran full length to terminate by the rear wheel instead of in a silencer box under the engine and the size of the front brakes had been increased to cope with the extra speed.

The next major step for BMW was the introduction in 1928 of two larger

Right

*What other manufacturer would house
the tool carrying box into one of the
engine/gearbox castings? OK so the tools
might get hot but it wouldn't matter as the
box hardly ever needed opening!*

engined machines to further supplement the range though it is worth noting that the R39 250 cc had been discontinued after 1926 and it was not until 1931 that another 'lightweight' was introduced. The new bigger models were the R62, a touring side-valve with 78 × 78 mm bore and stroke, 745 cc and the sporting R63 with the surprisingly modern 'over-square' dimensions of 83 × 68 mm, 735 cc. The side-valve produced 18 bhp at 3400 rpm and the overhead-valve a thumping 24 bhp at 4000 rpm – which was enough to give a top speed of around 80 mph.

It was the new 735 cc sports engine that gained BMW world-wide fame. For those were the days when speed records on land, sea and in the air, made headlines around the world and the men who set them became international heroes. The man in BMW's case was a small, shy rider from Munich named Ernst Henne. He had been a successful road racer and trials rider on BMW works machines since joining the team in 1926 and in 1928 had won the famous Targa Florio race in Sicily for them.

He had become interested in speed record attempts and, by coincidence, when he and his bride were honeymooning in Paris in 1929 the French press were full of stories about the battle between the two Englishmen, Oliver Baldwin and Bert Le Vack, who were seeking to improve the motorcycle world record on a stretch of 'route nationale' at Arpajon near Paris. Both were using mighty 1000 cc V-twin Tottenham-built JAP (J A Prestwich) engines in special frames. Eventually Le Vack won the day, setting a flying kilometre record at 129.08 mph and the mile at 128.34 mph riding his Brough Superior JAP.

Henne was convinced that he could break those records using the new short-stroke 735 cc engine. The factory already had experience of supercharging and his plan was to build a 'blown' machine and to attack the record on a straight but narrow and tree-lined section of the road from Munich to Ingolstadt. The Zoller supercharger was mounted above the gearbox and boosted the power of the racing engine from 36 bhp to over 70 bhp.

By September 1929 the machine was ready. Typical of Henne's attention to detail he wore a streamlined helmet and even had a streamlined 'tail' on his riding suit to reduce drag. The machine itself was low and light but carried no fairing. Ernst went out and first broke the mile record with an average of 134.68 mph and then shattered the kilometre figure at 134.75 mph. Then bureaucracy stepped in. The Federation Internationale Motocycliste officially confirmed the mile figure but refused the kilometre because that distance should have been attempted before the mile. So a few days later Henne returned and almost lost his life when the front wheel spindle came out of the fork ends when he was travelling at around 130 mph. Somehow he managed to control the BMW and brought it to a standstill without crashing: 'Fate was kind to me that day,' said the little Bavarian who went on to break many more records and to become a multi-millionaire selling BMW motorcycles and Mercedes cars.

Note how the R52's crown wheel and pinion assembly clamps over the abbreviated rear frame tubes, nicely engineered yet all wonderfully simple

Above
No excuses needed for showing another picture of Wallace Lambert's fabulous machine

Left
Half a cart type leaf spring controls the R52's front suspension, and note the unusual trailing wheel arrangement

A grand prix challenger

While Henne was blazing the trademark BMW across the world's headlines the factory was producing the new R11 and R16 750 cc models. These had first been shown at the London Motorcycle Show at Olympia in November 1928 but teething troubles led to hold-ups and the two new machines did not go into quantity production until late in 1929.

They looked very different from the R62 and R63 models they replaced. Gone were the duplex tubular loop frames used since the first BMW, the R32, was launched in 1923. In their place were pressed-steel frames which became known as the 'star' frames – though no one now seems to know why. One theory is that it is a shortened form of 'stark', the German word for strong.

Strong they may have been, but aesthetically pleasing they were not. They gave the new models a cumbersome, heavy appearance which did little to promote sales outside the home country. The basic duplex layout was retained with two pressed-steel loops replacing the tubes. They were joined by cross-members while the tubular fork legs were replaced by pressed-steel ones with the trailing link suspension controlled by leaf spring retainers.

The engines were virtually unchanged. The R11 was powered by the 745 cc side-valve twin giving 18 bhp at 3400 rpm while the sports R16 was fitted with the over-square 735 cc unit which produced 25 bhp at 4000 rpm. Both still had three-speed gearboxes with hand-change and BMW had still not adopted twist-grip throttles though these were introduced on the Series 11 models late in 1930.

By the end of 1929 a total of 22,000 flat-twin BMWs had been sold and the factory was prospering. For in addition to the two-wheelers they had moved into cars, building first the Austin Seven under licence (selling it as the Dixi) and then developing their own vehicles, as well as building an increased range of aero-engines.

Then came the Wall Street Crash of 1930 and the Depression. The German government responded by creating a new class for light motorcycles. The riders would not need a licence and they would not have to pay any road tax. To meet demand for this new class, BMW built and launched the R2 (the model numbering system having gone haywire after the R63) which was a single-cylinder overhead-valve 198cc (63 × 64 mm bore and stroke) engine with three-speed gearbox mounted in a lightweight pressed-steel frame. Power output was 6 bhp at 3500 rpm, later uprated to 8 bhp at 4500 rpm. It was utility transport and sold well, the factory building 15,207 before it was replaced in 1936.

The Depression hit the road-racing side of the business but Henne kept the speed flag flying. Early in 1930 he clocked 123.76 mph for the flying kilometre riding on a course across a frozen lake at Ostersund in Sweden. Spiked tyres were used but even so Henne remembered crashing when he went out for a second run. In August 1930 Joe Wright took his mighty 1000 cc supercharged OEC-Temple-JAP to Arpajon and raised the two-wheeler world record to 137.32 mph. Henne replied with 137.66 mph in September which prompted Wright to go to a new venue, a long straight road near Cork in Ireland where he averaged a stunning 150.74 mph.

Henne tried again at Neunkirchner in Austria in April 1931 and although he set a 750 cc record at 148.04 mph it was not until November 1933 that he finally managed to beat Wright's outright record. Then, at Tat in Hungary, he achieved a speed of 151.86 mph. He increased this at Gyon in Hungary in October 1934 with 152.90 mph when he also used a 500 cc engine to set a class record at 141.40 mph and from then on it was the new half-litre racing engine on which the factory concentrated. Henne had one last fling on the 750 cc in 1936 when he clocked 159.10 mph but it was with the 500 cc in a streamlined shell that he achieved 169.02 mph that year. He then went on to respond to Piero Taruffi's Gilera record of 170.37 mph by setting a world record of 173.69 mph in November 1937 which stood for nearly 14 years.

During the years of Henne's record-breaking the factory had been steadily developing the roadsters. The most important step was fitting the sports R16 with twin Fischer-Amal carburettors in 1932. This helped raise the power from 25 bhp to 33 bhp but the expensive R16 remained an enthusiast's mount and by the end of 1934 only 1106 had been built compared to 7500 of the far cheaper side-valve R11.

Behind the scenes work was in progress on a brand new 500 cc road racer. Hitler had come to power in January 1933 and realizing the morale and sale boosting kudos to be gained by sporting successes he encouraged German manufacturers to go racing – BMW, DKW and NSU leading the two-wheeled challenge.

The BMW engineers stuck to the basic layout of a flat twin but the bore and stroke was 66×72 mm, giving a capacity of 492 cc and the gearbox was a four-speeder with positive stop foot-change – by that time a standard fitting on the majority of sports machines, though not adopted by BMW until the launch of the sports R5 in 1936. The supercharger, mounted atop the gearbox in earlier competition machines was moved to the front of the crankcase and the valve gear was new. The pushrods of the earlier racers had been replaced by shaft- and bevel-driven camshafts.

There were two camshafts per cylinder but these operated the valves via short rockers so the engine was not a true double overhead-camshaft, and this same set-up was used on the Rennsport racers of the early 1950s. This engine, which in its earliest form probably produced around 55 bhp, was mounted in a new frame built in the traditional way with tubes. There was no rear springing but up front was an innovation – a telescopic fork with hydraulic damping. Crude telescopic forks had been tried before but this was the first

Above
*The late 1930's supercharged Racer used
only one side-mounted carburettor*

with internal oil damping which stopped any possible 'rocking' motion which
might occur at high speed when the coil springs inside the legs were working
hard.

The new racer made its debut at the high-speed, banked Avus circuit near
Berlin in June 1935 when the prototype was ridden by Ludwig 'Wiggerl'
Kraus. It was not a fairy-tale first appearance, however, for the race was won
by the Swede Ragnar Sunnqvist, on a works Husqvarna V-twin, averaging 107
mph. Surprisingly, slightly detuned versions of the supercharged engines were
used by the BMW-mounted German trophy team in the International Six
Days Trial that year – and they came through to win. A member of the team
that year was Georg Meier, soon to become famous as a road racer.

After the Avus outing BMW appear to have concentrated on development,
and preparing the bikes for the ISDT, for there were no more notable race

outings in 1935. But when the German season opened in 1936 with the Eilenriede meeting in a park in Hanover in April, BMW fielded Karl Gall and Otto Ley on the new supercharged racers and there was talk in the British press of the German team coming over for the Isle of Man TT. Nothing came of that and in Continental events the new BMWs proved fast but difficult to handle.

In the Swiss Grand Prix, Norton's Jimmy Guthrie won the 500 cc class with a lap record of 91.74 but BMW had the consolation of second place, Ley beating Kurt Mansfeld (DKW). Guthrie went on to win the 500 cc German Grand Prix at the Sachsenring and the big class at the Dutch TT but again Ley was second and on the very fast Dutch TT circuit it was Ley who clocked a lap record at 91.25 mph. The BMW was acknowledged to be the fastest 500 cc racing machine but the problem was to improve the handling so that the riders were not physically exhausted after the first few laps.

In Sweden, at the end of August 1936, the new BMW scored its first win when, on the fast Saxtorp circuit, Ley won the race from Gall with the European Champion Guthrie relegated to third place. This was the first time that he and his Norton had been beaten fair and square since Stanley Woods (Guzzi) won the 1935 Senior TT. Ley's average was 91.79 mph and he set a lap record of 93.70 mph.

The lessons being learned from the race development programme were quickly incorporated into the road machines. As early as 1935 the side-valve 745 cc R11 and the sporting overhead-valve R16 with 33 bhp engine had been fitted with telescopic forks and been re-launched as the R12 and the R17. The new forks were the first of telescopic design with hydraulic damping to be fitted to standard production motorcycles. Curiously though BMW were slow to up-date the transmission. It was true that the new models were fitted with a four-speed gearbox but it was still hand-change which hardly fitted in with the R17's sporting 90 mph image, and which had long been abandoned by other manufacturers of high performance motorcycles.

Georg Meier push starts his supercharged race bike

The competition mounts

To catch up with, and many will claim to get ahead of, their rivals BMW launched a completely new machine at the Berlin Motor Show in February 1936. This was the R5 and was powered by a re-designed 494 cc flat-twin engine. The 68 × 68 mm bore and stroke of the earlier 500 cc units was retained as was the pushrod valve operation, virtually all else was changed. To allow high revs and high performance to be achieved these were lighter and shorter than before and were operated by two camshafts, one on each side of the crankcase, rather than by one central shaft.

The cylinder heads were light alloy and the coil valve springs were replaced by racing style hairpin springs – concealed within massive rocker box covers.

First ever foreign machine winner of a Senior TT, this the actual supercharged bike on which Georg Meier won the 1939 Race

Power output was 24 bhp at 5800 rpm and to make the best use of this BMW at last fitted a four-speed positive stop gearbox – operated by a pedal on the left. To accommodate this the long aluminium footboards used on virtually all BMWs since the first R32 went on sale in 1923, were replaced by simple footrests.

Out too went the ungainly looking pressed-steel 'star' frame. The new R5 had a neat tubular duplex frame – an updated version of the type abandoned in favour of pressed steel some six years previously with the joints now welded instead of brazed. The telescopic front fork with nearly 4 in. of movement was fitted but there was no rear suspension – not even the supercharged factory racer had that in February 1936. A refinement to the forks was that the damping characteristics could be altered by a control mounted at the top of the nearside fork leg.

The R5 (which sold in England for £115, some £15 more than the

No excuses needed for showing the other side of 1939's near 90 mph average speed Senior TT winner

International Norton which had a comparable performance) was followed, in 1937, by BMW's first 600 cc machine, the R6. This was designed for the growing sidecar market (at that time over a quarter of all machines sold were hitched to sidecars to provide affordable family transport) and was powered by a 'slogger' side-valve engine with 70×78 mm bore and stroke to give an exact capacity of 596 cc. Peak power was a lowly 18 bhp at 4000 rpm but this was less important than lusty torque throughout the range.

The R6, apart from the engine, was identical to the sports R5 with a four-speed foot-change gearbox mounted in the new welded frame with telescopic forks. Activity in the single-cylinder market included the launch of two new models in 1937 – first the R20 with an 8 bhp engine (60×68 mm, 192 cc) mounted in a tubular frame with a cheaper version of telescopic fork and, later, the 342 cc R35. This was mainly built for the armed forces and replaced the 398 cc R4 built from 1932 to 1937. The 72×84 mm engine was coupled to a four-speed hand-change gearbox mounted in a pressed-steel frame but with the lightweight version of the telescopic fork replacing the blade type of the R4. In all over 30,000 R4 and R35 BMWs were built.

In February 1938 no less than five new models were on display at the Berlin Motor Show, four of them with the plunger rear suspension developed on the racing twins during the 1937 season. Top of the range was a new 600 cc sports model, the R66. Surprisingly, this new sports engine was not based on the R5 although it did retain the hairpin valve springs. Bore and stroke were the same as the side-valve of the same capacity at 70×78 mm but the power was up from the 18 bhp of the 'slogger' to an impressive 30 bhp at 5300 rpm which was enough to give a top speed of over 90 mph in solo form and 70 mph when hitched to a sports sidecar.

The sports R5 was replaced by the rear-sprung R51 while the R6 with spring heel was redesignated the R61. The biggest of the twin-cylinder foursome was the R71 powered by an uprated version of the trusty 78×78 mm, 745 cc side-valve engine. It was the last side-valve unit to be built by the German factory and was phased out in 1941.

Completing the Berlin Show quintet was the R23, a 247 cc single-cylinder (BMW's first true quarter-litre since the demise of the R39 in 1926) with square bore and stroke of 68×68 mm which produced a sprightly 10 bhp at 5400 rpm. This was mounted in a neat tubular frame with the lightweight telescopic fork which lacked the hydraulic damping of the units fitted to the bigger machines.

On the racing front BMW built on the success of Otto Ley and Karl Gall in the 1936 Swedish Grand Prix. First Gall won the 500 cc class of the 1937 Dutch TT at 92.27 mph and with a lap record of 95.01 mph he outpaced the Nortons of Jimmy Guthrie and Harold Daniell. In Switzerland, the Grand Prix of Europe that year, the superior handling of the British singles told and Guthrie won from team-mate Freddie Frith. Guthrie won again at the Belgian Grand

Meier the Maestro in action again on the Isle of Man TT Course

Prix but was then killed when he crashed on the last lap of the German Grand Prix at the Sachsenring. Gall took over to win while Otto Ley won the Swedish Grand Prix and Jock West the Ulster to make it four out of seven major grand prix wins that year.

The first race of the 1938 classic season was the Isle of Man TT and BMW fielded a three-man team of veteran Gall, rising star Georg Meier who had replaced Ley and England's Jock West who had ridden a solitary works machine into sixth place in the previous year's 500 cc Senior TT. But things went badly for the German team. First Gall was eliminated by a crash during practice and then Meier was left on the line when a thread stripped while changing from the warming-up to racing plugs.

West battled on but could only finish fifth in a race won by Harold Daniell on a re-vamped works Norton (now with a telescopic fork but without the hydraulic damping of the BMW unit), who set a lap record at 91.00 mph that remained unbroken for 12 years. At the Belgian Grand Prix Meier was the winner of the 259-mile race at 90.39 mph but even on the fast Spa-Francorchamps circuit the Norton was a formidable rival and it was Freddie Frith who set a lap record at 96.94 mph to finish second ahead of West (BMW).

Nortons won in Geneva where the Swiss Grand Prix was held that year, with Daniell finishing ahead of Frith. But the British factory missed the Dutch TT, possibly because they feared the long straights connected by slow corners which made the circuit ideal for supercharged multi-cylinder machines. Meier won the race there though only after the Italian Dorino Serafini had crashed while leading on a four-cylinder Gilera. Meier won again at the German Grand Prix, that year's European Grand Prix, with Daniell and Frith on Nortons taking second and third places.

By the time the rivals met again in Ulster Joe Craig of Norton had found some more speed for his riders. Frith set the fastest practice lap at 98.80 mph and then led the race by an ever-increasing margin until a slide-off. Team-mate Daniell took over only to be forced to retire when a wheel-bearing broke up letting West (BMW) through to win.

John Surtees tries the 1939 TT winning bike out at the 1989 Brands Hatch Superprix

Georg and Frau Meier, Walter Zeller, THE bike, and various other racing greats paying tribute to Karl Gall at his memorial at Ballaugh on the TT Course, the spot where he crashed and was killed practising for the 1939 race

With the war clouds gathering and with military orders to fulfil, Norton then pulled out of racing leaving BMW to battle with Gilera for the 500 cc honours. Meier won the 1939 Senior TT at the record average of 89.38 mph with team-mate West second despite the fact that the veteran Gall had been killed when he crashed during practice.

In those days all the bikes were weighed and Meier's BMW was the lightest bike in the Senior TT at only 302 lbs, compared to the 336 lbs of Frith's Norton (a 1938 works machine that he rode into third place) and the 404 lbs of the massive supercharged four-cylinder AJS of Walter Rusk. Meier went on to make it three in a row by winning the Dutch TT and the Belgian Grand Prix where he lapped the modified course at 100.63 mph. This was the first time the 'ton' lap had been achieved in a classic . . . Walter Rusk's lap at over 100 mph in the Ulster came later in the year.

Meier and BMW, in fact, had two 100 mph laps to their credit before the Ulster for the Bavarian lapped at 100.83 mph in the Swedish Grand Prix but then crashed while striving to beat Serafini (Gilera) who went on to win. This injury put Meier out of the 1939 German Grand Prix where Serafini won again, as he did at the Ulster Grand Prix, the last major race before war broke out in September 1939.

Just how fast was the 1939 supercharged BMW twin? Jock West reckoned that it developed about 68 bhp and had a top speed of very close to 140 mph on Isle of Man gearing. It was the end of an era.

The road to recovery

By the time Europe went to war in 1939 BMW had produced a staggering total of 160,000 machines ranging from the 192 cc R20 to the mighty 745 cc twins. All shared the same basic layout with the crankshaft in-line with the wheels, driving the gearbox through a car type clutch and then with shaft drive to the rear wheel.

For solo work the German Army used the 342 cc single-cylinder R35 and a military version of the R12 with 745 cc side-valve twin engine, in almost equal numbers. Over 30,000 of both types were built in the years immediately before and during the war. Both had the pressed-steel frame abandoned for the civilian market but they were fitted with telescopic forks.

However, the most famous war-time BMW was the mighty Wehrmacht R75, a true colossus among sidecar outfits which weighed 900 lbs when fuelled up and ready to go. The added weight of the three-man crew, machine gun, ammunition and other stores bringing the total close to a ton! The R75 was built in answer to a specification issued to manufacturers in 1938. The army wanted a 'go anywhere' motorized infantry vehicle to take the place of the horse.

BMW built the prototype R75 in 1939 and it finally went into production in 1941. It was designed as a complete vehicle, not as a motorcycle and sidecar, and could not be split and ridden solo. The engine was a detuned overhead-valve 745 cc (78 × 78 mm) with a low compression ratio which developed 26 bhp at 4000 rpm with plenty of power throughout the range. This was coupled to a foot-change four-speed gearbox with hand-operated over-drive to give eight forward speeds and two reverse. In addition, there was shaft drive from the rear bevel housing across to the sidecar wheel with a differential so that the R75 always had two-wheel drive just as you have on a car. When the going got slippery there was a differential lock to prevent one wheel spinning.

The 16 in. wheels were shod with wide section tyres and the brakes, on all three wheels, were of 10 in. diameter and were hydraulically operated. The top speed was 60 mph and 18,000 were built before they were superceded by a four-wheel Volkswagen jeep-type vehicle later in the war.

In 1942 all motorcycle production was moved to the nearby Eisenach factory, absorbed into the BMW group when production of the Austin-inspired Dixi light car was taken over in the late 1920s. Both Eisenach and the parent

An ex-Desert War R75 outfit, complete and original except for the lack of a machine gun!

The Russians liberated the R75 design during World War 2, and then produced their own version known variously as the Ural, Cossack or Dnieper

Munich factory, where aero-engines were designed and built (notably for the very fast Focke-Wulfe 190 fighter and for the triple-engined Junkers 52 transport), were heavily bombed. Munich was particularly hard hit and on 11 April 1945 Hitler tried to finish the job for the Allies when he issued orders from his Berlin bunker that what remained of the factory should be destroyed to prevent anything useful falling into the hands of the enemy.

Kurt Donath and Arthur Scholl, two surviving board members (Franz Joseph Popp, an Austrian had been managing director from 1917 until he retired in 1942), decided to ignore the order and save what they could. It was precious little and recovery was further complicated by the fact that the Eisenach factory lay within the Russian zone while anything left at the

Munich plant was subject to examination and, if useful, removed to the USA by the Americans who occupied Bavaria.

It was 1919 all over again! And, as at the end of World War 1, BMW made what they could – pots and pans, bakery equipment, agricultural machinery – to assist Germany's post-war recovery and keep the factory and the workforce busy. Initially they were not allowed to make motorcycles and in any case they had no facilities to do so. What had survived the war was in Eisenach behind what was soon to become known as the 'iron curtain'. There were not even any drawings left. They had been destroyed in the bombing.

When the Allies became favourable to suggestions that BMW be allowed to resume motorcycle production, to fulfil a strong demand for transport, pre-war bikes were stripped and new drawings made from the component parts. The first 'new' machines were built in December 1948. This was the R24 with a single-cylinder 247 cc engine up-rated from the 10 bhp of the old R23 to 12 bhp at 5600 rpm but otherwise identical to the pre-war bike. Nearly 10,000 were produced in 1949 and in 1950 it was replaced by the R25 with the plunger rear suspension fitted to the twins in pre-war days.

It took longer to get the more complicated twins back into production. First to appear was the R51/2 which, as the model number makes clear, was a slightly modified version of the R51 introduced in 1938. The engine was 494 cc (68 × 68 mm) mounted in a plunger-sprung frame with the hydraulic telescopic front fork. This went on sale in 1950 and a year later it was joined by the first new twin since the war – the R67. Built for sidecar work this had a new engine with 72 × 73 mm bore and stroked (594 cc) which produced 26 bhp at 5500 rpm. A notable innovation was the fitting of a two-leading-shoe front brake, a definite asset when trying to stop a heavily loaded sidecar outfit from speed.

The 494 cc model was further refined and the R51/3, with an improved engine, was launched at the Amsterdam Show in February 1951. The power unit had been cleaned up with the magneto and generator all neatly tucked away, improvements had been made to the valve gear and the rocker-box covers re-designed.

Later the same year the first genuine 100 mph production BMW was the star of the Frankfurt Motor Cycle Show. This was the R68, the sporting flagship that enthusiasts had been hoping for. It was powered by a re-designed 594 cc engine (72 × 73mm) uprated to produce 35 bhp and to rev to 7000 rpm. Compression ratio was up from the 5.6:1 of the 'cooking' 594 cc to 7.5:1, valve sizes had been increased annd bigger twin Bing carburettors fitted (up from 22 to 26 mm).

Germany had been re-admitted to international motorcycle sport, the German economy was booming and motorcycle sales were rocketing as a new breed of affluent workers expanded their horizons and took to the roads of Europe.

The 500 cc telefork R51 of 1952, albeit now with flashing indicators to suit today's traffic

R 25/3 TOURING MODEL 250 c.c., 13 H.P.
with BMW sidecar "Standard"

Innovations on BMW single cylinder motorcycles: Increased engine power; extended exhaust system for regularly cool air duct; intense silencing of noise produced by gears, aspiration and exhaust systems; improved and especially smooth-acting clutch; telescope fork with hydraulic shock absorption; more active springing; highly polished 18° light metal rims; enlarged light metal full width brakes; saddle tank with toolbox to be locked laterally; stoplight.

Sidecar oscillating axle and boat with soft rubber suspension; connection by four ball points; transportation of 3 persons admissible.

TOURING MODEL 250 c.c. – 13 H.P. **R 25/3**

R 51/3 TOURING-SPORTS MODEL

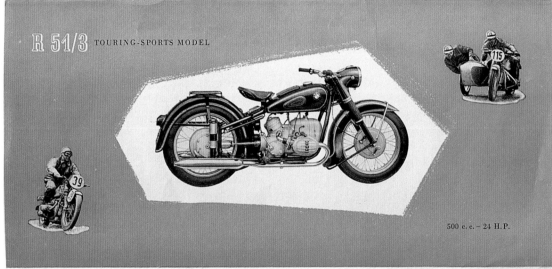

500 c.c. – 24 H.P.

R 67/2 TOURING-SPORTS MODEL 600 c.c., 28 H.P.
with BMW oscillating axle sidecar "Spezial"

Innovations on all BMW twin cylinder models: Intense absorption of noise caused by gears, aspiration and exhaust systems; improved and especially smooth acting clutch; highly polished light metal rims, enlarged light metal full width brakes; stoplight; Sidecar oscillating axle and boat with soft rubber suspension; additional telescope shock absorber can be fitted; essentially improved riding capacities of combination by hydraulic oil brake for sidecar wheel.

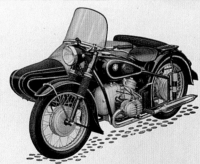

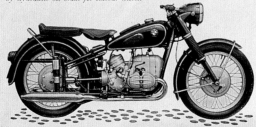

SPORTS MODEL 600 c.c. – 35 H.P. **R 68**

Now also with sidecar connection by four ball points.

A slightly later American specification R25, with a US option red painted gas tank

Drawing admiring glances wherever it goes this R51/3 (and Steib sidecar) is registered in Germany

Post-war racing

Racing in Germany resumed almost as soon as the war was over. Many of the pre-war works machines and a surprisingly large number of the top riders had survived including 1939 Senior TT winner Georg Meier and on his blown BMW he was soon battling it out with the supercharged NSU twin which was being developed when war broke out. Initially the German riders were restricted to racing in national events and could not contest the World Championship series inaugurated by the Fédération Internationale Motocycliste in 1949.

All this changed in 1951 when the German federation was admitted back into the fold. This posed problems, for the FIM had banned superchargers and it meant that the German factories would have to develop new machines if they wanted to compete. The initial BMW response was to race the pre-war machines without the supercharger. Riding one of these, Meier, by this time aged 41, chased the Norton team when they contested the German Grand Prix at Solitude near Stuttgart in 1951. Mounted on the brilliant new 'featherbed' racers the British team of Geoff Duke, Ken Kavanagh, Jack Brett and Johnny Lockett took the first four places but the veteran Meier on a ten-year-old BMW, shorn of its blower, was only just behind fourth placed Lockett.

A young German on a second works BMW finished sixth behind Meier. His name was Walter Zeller and although Meier continued racing in German events until 1953 it was Zeller who became the Munich factory's number one for international events. 1952 was a year of development on the racing front. Zeller and Hans Baltisberger rode in a few events on new experimental racers but achieved little international success though, with Meier, they proved formidable in German races.

At the ultra-fast egg-shaped Grenzlandring Zeller won at an average of 117.60 mph while Meier upped the lap record to a startling 123.70 mph. At Schotten Meier again set the fastest lap and won from Zeller with Ray Amm (Norton) third, while at the Stadtparkrennen in Hamburg the BMW team took a 1–2–3 with Meier winning fron Zeller and Baltisberger. It was much the same story in 1953 when Meier, by that time aged 43, retired after winning the 500 cc German championship. The British weekly *Motor Cycling* commented in a review of the racing year: 'BMW did not prove a force to be reckoned with . . . perhaps the efforts of this famous factory were mainly exploratory, for no team was regularly entered and experimental work was constantly proceeding.'

The result of this work became clear when BMW produced a batch of 25 racing machines for sale in 1954. This was the famous Rennsport (racing-sport) model. BMW had sold small batches of 500 cc racing machines in pre-war days but these had all been powered by pushrod engines and were tuned

Above

Works Rennsport mounted Walter Zeller at the Gooseneck on the TT Circuit and en route to fourth place in the 1956 Senior Race, and second overall in that year's World Championships, which was BMW's best placing in this event

Previous page

The immortal Geoff Duke rode for BMW in 1958, and finished fourth in the World Title, though it wasn't the happiest liaison

sports models rather than out-and-out racers. The first was the R5SS in 1937 followed by the rear-sprung R51SS in 1938 and the R41RS in 1939. This last machine was a more serious effort to match the rival Manx Norton with power increased to 36 bhp and top speed of 115 mph. Curiously, despite the success of the factory trials and racing machines none of these 'over the counter' racers were supercharged.

Like the pre-war racers the new Rennsport was only sold to selected riders but unlike the earlier models it was a true replica of the latest factory machine. The very compact engine had a bore and stroke of 66 × 72 mm (492 cc) and breathed through two 30 mm Fischer-Amal carburettors. Surprisingly, the batch as built had only a four-speed gearbox but these were later modified to five-speeds by owners who wanted to be competitve. Power output was 55 bhp at 8000 rpm with the engine able to rev to 9000 rpm in the gears.

The Rennsport was a difficult machine to ride. Because the cylinders stuck out on either side the engine had to be mounted high in the frame to give clearance while cornering, and this in turn raised the centre of gravity. Frontal

area was also greater than with a single-cylinder and yet another handicap was the torque-twist effect of the longitudinally placed crankshaft – when the rider accelerated hard or shut off from high speed the machine tried to keel over in sympathy with the torque reaction; all rather unnerving and requiring a very different riding technique to 'normal' machines.

The frame probably did not help. Short and high it had the theoretically superior but relatively unproven pivoted-fork Earles type at the front and orthodox swinging fork at the rear with the drive shaft concealed in the right-side leg. But the marvellous engine more than made up for the problematic handling and in the right hands (initially Gerold Klinger of Austria, Hans Riedelbauch and Ernst Hiller of Germany and later Dickie Dale of England and Jack Forrest of Australia) the Rennsport dominated the 500 cc class of the lesser international meetings held in Europe in 1957 and 1958.

By this time the majority of Rennsport owners had given up trying to master them and had taken a quick profit by selling them to sidecar competitors. For while the BMW made a tricky solo machine that lovely

Double Sidecar Racing World Champions Willy Schneider and Hans Strauss winning the 1958 Sidecar TT. BMW's Rennsports have long dominated sidecar racing scoring an impressive 19 World Titles

Walter Zeller's 1954 Works Rennsport 500

Zeller (No 2 second left) awaiting the off

engine-gearbox unit was perfect for the three-wheeler class. The works supported riders had shown the way. Little Willi Noll and passenger Fritz Cron led the charge when they overcame the Norton duo of Eric Oliver/Les Nutt and Cyril Smith/Stan Dibben to win the 1954 Sidecar World Championship.

Compatriots Willi Faust/Karl Remmert took over in 1955 to continue a BMW dominance that was to last for nearly 20 years. It was a different story in the solo class. Walter Zeller was the lone fully supported factory rider and in 1954 and 1955 he rode the factory development 500 cc racer mainly in German events. In the latter year the factory was encouraged by Zeller taking second place to Geoff Duke (Gilera) in the German Grand Prix at the Nürburgring and this prompted them to field Zeller in the 1956 series. The bore and stroke of the engine had been changed – first from 66×72 mm to 68×68 mm (which raised peak revs to 9500 rpm and the power output to around 60 bhp) and finally to well over-square at 70×64 mm with a 10,000 rpm limit and 65 bhp.

The wealthy young Bavarian started the season with a fourth place in the Isle of Man Senior TT, handicapped by a last-minute decision not to use streamlining because of the strong winds that prevailed that day, then improved to finish a magnificent second in the Dutch TT, beaten only by John Surtees (MV Agusta). The next weekend Zeller again took second place, at the Belgian Grand Prix, and despite disappointments in Germany and Ireland and a sixth place in the final round in Italy, Zeller finished second to Surtees in the 1956 500 cc World Championship.

Zeller and BMW tried again in 1957 but that year Gilera were back in strength and the best he could do were two third places, in the German Grand Prix and Dutch TT. The motorcycle market was in recession and BMW were forced to cut back on the factory racing project. Realizing that he stood no chance against the Italian multis and facing up to his responsibilities towards the family steel business, Zeller retired at the end of the 1957 season.

As luck would have it he may have quit a year too early. For late that year Gilera, Moto Guzzi and Mondial quit racing. This left only MV Agusta to beat – and a lot of top riders without works machines. Geoff Duke took over the Zeller machine but never got the best out of it, ditching it in favour of a Norton before the end of the season. Dickie Dale, on a suitably updated Rennsport, was more successful. Picking up points with regular placings he took third place in the 500 cc World Championship. Then, as the competition grew tougher, the solo BMW racers faded from the scene leaving it to the BMW sidecar outfits to carry the famous blue and white quartered trade mark on the race circuits of Europe.

Portrait of Max Deubel's all-conquering sidecar race engine

Left

*1964 runners up and 1965 World
Champions, Fritz Schneidegger and John
Robinson photographed at the time at
Brands Hatch*

Above

*Hans Luthringshauser and J Cusnik
finished runners up in the 1972 World
Sidecar Championship*

Above
Dickie Dale during 1958 and en route to a posthumous 3rd place in that year's 500 cc Solo World Title

Right
Still winning into the 1980s, Kurt Liebmann just keeps his Rennsport ahead of Dave Roper's Matchless G.50 at Daytona in 1982

The marketplace

While the racing activities were capturing the sporting headlines the technical staff at Munich were patiently developing the classic flat twin roadsters. A major step forward was the adoption, in 1955, of the race-style frame with Earles front forks and, more importantly from a rider's comfort point of view, the swinging fork rear suspension. Two models with the new frame were launched at the Brussels Motor Show in January 1955 – a 'bread and butter' 500 cc (68 × 68 mm, 494 cc) which developed 26 bhp at 5800 rpm and a new flagship – the R69. This replaced the R68 and retained the 594 cc 35 bhp engine to give a genuine top speed of over 100 mph.

These were quality machines engineered to the highest standards and their prices reflected this. In England, where a punitive import tax further increased the price, the R50 sold for £378 and the R69 for £492. By comparison the equally fast 650 cc BSA Golden Flash was listed at £248 while the even faster Triumph Tiger 110 cost £254. In America the price differential was not so distorted and the USA became BMW's major export market.

Both new models had 18 in. wheels in place of 19 in., twin leading-shoe front brakes and a dual-seat was offered as an optional extra. Standard models retained the famous sprung rubber saddle though the sporting R69 had a race-style pad bolted to the back which could be used by the rider to adopt a racing crouch or to carry a pillion passenger. To cater for sidecar enthusiasts a 'softer' 594 cc machine was added to the range in 1956. Code-named the R60 this replaced the plunger-framed R67/3 and from that machine inherited the 594 cc 28 bhp engine.

By this time the motorcycle industry around the world was in deep recession. Production of cheap family cars had at last caught up with demand and makers of motorcycles could no longer sell all they could make. In 1957 three famous German manufacturers pulled out of the market – DKW, Adler and Horex. BMW production fell from a peak of 29,699 machines in 1954 to 5500 in 1957. The motorcycle side of BMW was, beyond argument, saved by the American market. There, by lucky chance, interest in sports machines was just beginning to boom and during one period no less than 85 per cent of flat-twin BMWs were exported to the USA.

The car side of the business was in trouble too. The luxury V8 did not sell well while the utility Isetta 'bubble car', produced with either three or four wheels according to the market it was aimed at (either a single rear wheel or two close together) with its 250 cc single-cylinder engine was just too austere for the booming European economy. For a time BMW tottered on the verge of bankruptcy, heavily subsidized by the Bavarian authorities. In 1959 Mercedes-Benz came in with a takeover bid but by that time things were looking a little

brighter and the bid was rejected. Just a few years later these two famous factories dominated the European luxury car market with vehicles of incredible complexity – and price!

BMW's first successful step to recovery was the introduction of a light, sports four-wheeler powered by a suitably modified flat-twin motorcycle engine. Named the BMW700 it caught the sporty mood of the time and at last the Munich factory had a best-seller. Motorcycle sales had continued to increase in America prompting BMW to introduce four new models in a launch at the Nürburgring in August 1960.

The basic 494 cc R50 was little changed but became the R50/2 while the power of the revised R60 (the R60/2) was increased to 30 bhp. The real changes came in the sports section where the 594 cc R69 was replaced by two models so that speed enthusiasts had a choice of capacities. The smaller machine was the R500S with a high-revving 68 × 68mm, 494 cc engine which

The rarer than rare R69 Sportster, of which BMW only ever built around 1330. This 1961 version is one of the very last, and what's more it is fitted with one of Steib's fabulous 501 sidecars

produced 35 bhp at 7650 rpm. Those who preferred a bigger engine were offered the R69S with the power of the 594 cc engine increased from 35 to 42 bhp at 7000 rpm.

To get the best out of these high-revving performance engines the two S models were fitted with close-ratio gearboxes. The chassis, with Earles forks and rear swinging fork remained little changed but the 1960 bikes could easily be recognized by the Hella indicator lamps fitted to the ends of the handlebar. The R69S proved a great success and over 11,000 were built in a nine-year production span but the very high revving R50S was phased out after only two years in which time only 1634 were sold.

On the sporting front the London BMW dealer, MLG, first entered an R69 in the Thruxton 500-Mile Race (for production sports machines) in 1958 when the bike finished third. They returned in 1959 to win, ridden by Peter Darvill and John Lewis, and later that year scored an even more outstanding success by triumphing in the truly arduous Barcelona 24-hour race. This was run on a dangerous, twisting circuit around Montjuic Park where the 1992 Olympic Games were held. The circuit could hardly have been less suitable for the big and heavy BMW and Darvill, now partnered by Bruce Daniels, outlasted the swifter, nimbler opposition to win.

With some help from the factory (the machine was the ideal test-bed for possible speed modifications being tried for the R69S) MLG continued in 1960 and again won both the Thruxton and Barcelona events. These performances finally buried any ideas that BMW motorcycles were only suitable for touring. Another sporting milestone was achieved in 1961 when an MLG team of four rode a specially prepared and partly streamlined R69S at the Montlhéry circuit near Paris and broke the 24-hour record at 109.24 mph (covering 2622 miles). The riders were Sid Mizen, Ellis Boyce, George Catlin and John Holder and the record stood for 16 years.

The sporting publicity coupled to BMW's reputation for first-class engineering and a continuing upsurge in sales of high-performance machines both in America and later in Europe, led to a period of stagnation – there was no need to change things when all the machines the factory could build were sold. In fact the only major option during the mid 1960s was the introduction of long-travel telescopic forks on the bikes for sale in the United States. Introduced in 1967 these models were designated the R50US, R60US and the R69US.

Behind the scenes, though, there was plenty going on. Two challenges had to be faced. First, the car side of the business was so successful that a great deal more room was needed and the obvious solution seemed to be to take over the space occupied by the adjoining motorcycle factory. The second was that towards the end of the decade the existing twins began to look dated compared to the new wave of British and Japanese superbikes. In 1969 BMW called a major press conference to announce their plans for the 1970s.

Famous for his engineering ability within Earles Fork BMW circles, Graham Crate poses with his personalised R69 and Steib

Above

*Unlike its successor, the R69
enjoyed a manual advance and retard
magneto ignition control as well as an
automatic arrangement, making this
model the sidecarist's first choice because
they could retard a little more when the
brake was heavily laden, if struggling up
hills*

Right

*Semi-bird's eye view of the rare R69 and
Steib with modified Craven luggage
carrying equipment*

Opposite

*BMW's incongruous little front opening
Isetta bubble car. It was not wise to park
these too close to anything else or the
driver might not be able to get out or in*

A mid-1960s touring R60/2 model still on the road some 30 years on

Some battle scars to show for this 1965 model R60/2's 70,000+ miles of continuous and reliable service

Opposite

Clever, the Germans – few people would realise that this era's BMWs carried their tool roll within the fuel tank, all locked and hidden away incidentally behind a dummy knee grip

Left

Some tool kit too! Certainly far superior to most

Below

The Supersports R69S Production Racer was only externally distinguishable from the R60 Tourer by fewer fins on the engine rocker cover, larger bore carburettors and a larger air cleaner pan. The extra timing cover bulge hid a special crankshaft vibration damper, and finally a hydraulic (rather than friction disc) steering damper assembly

Above
*Don Morley's well used and much loved
R69S dates from 1963*

Right
*The high revving 69S's speedometer
advised changing from first gear at 40
mph, second at 60 mph and third at 85
mph, whereas the Touring R60's
instrument suggested 31, 47 and 67 mph
respectively*

Left
The 250s were of exactly the same comfort and quality, and what's more also shared many of the bigger bike's components, which in turn meant that they were frankly rather underpowered

Below
Pip Harris, who was one of the world's top Rennsport sidecar racing exponents of the 1960s, also often raced this standard looking R69S outfit as here in 1963

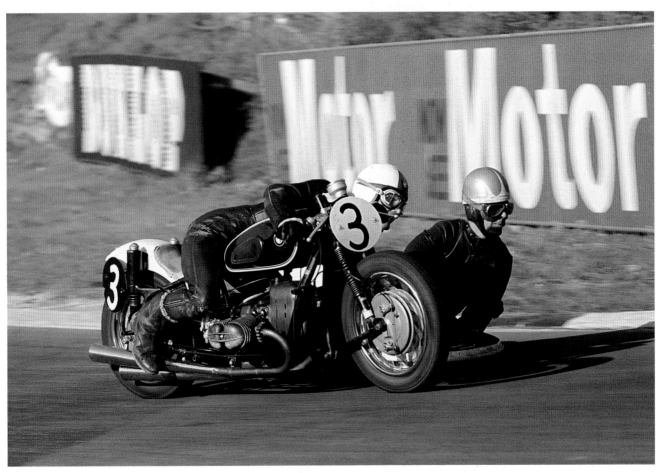

Above

Prior to 1970 there were several saddle options ranging from the dual seat through to the horrendously expensive-to-replace rubber, or coil spring sprung separate saddles whose comforts are generally preferred amongst BMW cognoscente

Left

A pre-tele fork American spec R27 photographed in Florida

Right

Bruce Daniels racing at Silverstone during 1961 on the 1960 Barcelona 24-hour winning bike

Developing a healthy future

The answer to the space problem was to move the motorcycle side of BMW from its traditional home in Munich to a new factory in Spandau, a suburb of Berlin famous for the manufacture of machine guns used by the German forces in two world wars. The factory there officially opened in September 1969 and at the same time a completely new and re-styled range of three machines was launched to replace the Earles fork models.

The newcomers had been carefully styled to combine an aggressively 'macho' look with flowing lines. The new frame was a near copy of the famous Norton featherbed with a neater, more modern rear end and the long-travel telescopic fork at the front. A new, deeper tank and upswept sports silencers coupled to a slimmer dual-seat and re-styled mudguards (made of plastic) carried the styling through.

A lot of work had been done on the engines too. Learning from the high-performance car engines they had developed, the BMW design team built the new flat-twins with plain main bearings and big-ends – gone were the roller bearings used for close on 50 years. Another car touch was the adoption of a full flow replaceable paper-element oil filter. The cylinder barrels were now light alloy with shrunk in cast-iron liners and to simplify production the three different capacity engines all shared a common crankcase and internals – the only things that differed were the cylinder bore, pistons and the cylinder heads and carburettors.

Another feature of the new engine was that it was 'taller' and now filled the gap between power unit and tank – a move to please the stylists. This extra space was used to house another innovation – an electric starter as well as a built-in air-filter. The new models were dubbed the 5-series and the three capacities available were the R50/5 496 cc with 67×70.6 mm bore and stroke and a power output of 32 bhp at 6400 rpm; the R60/5 599 cc (73.5×70.6 mm) with 40 bhp at 6400 rpm and the R75/5 745 cc (82×70.6 mm) producing 50 bhp at 6200 rpm. Top speeds were said to be 98, 104 and 105 mph respectively.

The new machines were a great success and no alterations were made until 1973. Then the 6-series appeared with a slightly longer rear swinging arm to aid stability and, more importantly, a five-speed gearbox. By this time some rival manufacturers were offering bigger machines and in 1974 BMW answered the challenge by producing two 898 cc engined models – the touring R90/6 with 60 bhp and the impressive sports R90S with 67 bhp power output. Again the engine was the basic unit with 70.6 mm stroke but now the bore was a massive 90 mm.

Both had the five-speed gearbox and disc front brakes – the R90S had a double disc set-up to handle the 120 mph top speed it could achieve; propelled by the new 67 bhp engine which breathed through 38 mm Dell'Orto

Something old, something new: International Six Days' Trial exponent Herbert Schek with the 1970/71 Works prepared 740 off-road BMW

The legendary Hans Fritzel on the Works ISDT bike in the 1979 event in Germany

carburettors and fitted, as standard, with a small fairing and windscreen. The 'softer' R90/6 had a lower compression ratio and smaller carburettors but still produced 60 bhp. At the same time as the new, bigger models were introduced the 496 cc R50/6 was dropped from the range (so that for the first time since 1923 there was no longer a 500 cc machine available) and the R60/6 and R75/6 were equipped with single disc front brakes, an option previously restricted to police models.

Three years later, in the autumn of 1976, the 7-series was announced. The two smaller models had only cosmetic changes but the size of the 898 cc engine was lifted to 980 cc by increasing the bore size from 90 to 94 mm. Thus the R90/6 was replaced by the R100/7 tourer and the R90S by the R100S.. This was no longer the flagship of the range for BMW took this opportunity to introduce the super-sports R100RS which, powered by a 70 bhp verison of the basic unit and aided by a comprehensive streamlined fairing (the first fitted as standard to a production motorcycle), gave a top speed of 125 mph and a 0–60 mph time of 4.6 sec. An addition to the range was the R80/7 with 797 cc

engine (84.8 × 70.6 mm). This had a low compression engine and was developed for markets where premium grade fuel was not available.

This new range proved an outstanding success and during 1977 the factory produced a new record of 31,515 bikes. But not everyone wanted a 600 cc or bigger machine and to answer dealer requests for a smaller capacity motorcycle, including a strong plea from the German agents who wanted a lower powered bike to get within a new under-27 bhp insurance class, the factory produced a smaller capacity model in March 1978.

Basically, the existing engine was used but the 70.6 mm stroke common to all previous machines since the launch of the 5-series in 1969, was changed to 61.5 mm. Coupled to a 70 mm bore this gave a capacity of 473 cc with the detuned German version producing 27 bhp at 6500 rpm while an export model delivered 35 bhp – but was never exported to America. This engine was mounted in a slightly lighter chassis and at the same time the R65 was added to the range This had basically the same short-stroke engine but with 82 mm bores to raise the capacity to 649 cc with 45 bhp on tap at 7250 rpm – later uprated to 50 bhp.

Above

The altogether new and much lighter drum-braked R60/5 of 1970, as directly developed from the company's ISDT machines

Overleaf

The large capacity R90/6 Tourer with the optional extra (double) front disc brake

Although neither machine was glamorous they both proved a good 'bread and butter' line for the BMW dealers and nearly 60,000 were sold before they were both phased out seven years later. Later in the year these models first appeared (1978), BMW introduced a touring version of the sports R100RS. Known as the R100RT, it was fitted with a more comprehensive streamlining which allowed the rider to cruise sitting up rather than crouching as on the R100RS. Both models had the neat cast alloy spoked wheels first introduced when the R100RS was launched.

The same year the R100/7 was replaced by the R100T, which was basically the same but with the power upped from 60 to 65 bhp. The R100S received the same treatment and was re-catalogued as the R100CS – now with 70 bhp. Since then the much loved twins have been steadily improved without any really radical changes.

The last really different boxer twin produced by BMW was the R80G/S first shown in September 1980. Based on machines developed by the factory for long-distance trials, including the International Six Days Trial, the R80G/S was an aggressively styled sports machine designed primarily for fast road work but with enough ground clearance to make it suitable for off-road 'green laning'. Features included bigger wheels, a high level exhaust system with the

Below and right

Arguably the prettiest and best boxer twin BMW ever made, the mid-1970s semi Production Racing R90S

twin pipes siamezed into a single silencer and single sided rear swing arm in place of the conventional fork.

BMW had long since broken away from the pre-war black with white-lining finish but the R80G/S (the G/S is short for *Gelandestrasse* which translates as cross-country and road) was the most flamboyant BMW yet with a brilliant white tank and a flame red seat. It proved an outstandingly successful motorcycle and in 1981 Frenchman Hubert Auriol, on a factory bike, won the toughest rally of them all – the Paris-Dakar. Two years later he repeated this success riding a works GS with a near 1000 cc engine.

But the BMW technical staff had long realized that something more than a constant up-rating of the faithful twin was needed if the BMW range of motorcycles was to have a healthy future. What was needed was a completely new design that would incorporate all the latest technical advances learned by BMW in their quest for excellence in the luxury car market. The project to design and build this machine, code-named the K model, started early in 1978.

Overleaf
Helmut Dähne – seen here on the start line – and Hans Otto Butenuth shared this R90S to win the 1976 Production TT

Above and right

BMWs dominated the mid to late 1970s American Production Racing scene with R90S machines ridden by Reg Pridmore and Ron Peirce. The latter is seen here winning at Laguna Seca

Laguna Seca 1977, and the BMW race
camp is split between the older 90s (right)
and new 1000 cc Seven Series R100s (left)

Goodwood 1976, and the UK launch of the 1000 cc fully faired R100RS (left) seen here with that year's equivalent R100/7 and R75/7 models

Above and right

An R100RT Tourer of 1979 with the optional driving lights built into the fairing

BMW's limited edition 'Motosport' colour scheme arguably suited the R100RS rather better than the original plain silver blue

Above and right

1982, and the new R80RT with cast alloy wheels

Police forces the world over loved the T80RT but, as here, often preferred to retain the earlier style wire wheels

Much underrated, the higher revving and decidedly nimble late 1970s onwards short-wheel base R65

Above
*One of the resulting mono-shock 80GS
semi off-road machines*

Right
*The 750 cc BMWs as used in the 1979
ISDT provided most of the technology for
the later R65s and the coming big trail
bikes*

Above and right
Red always seems to suit BMWs as this 80GS shows

Opposite
Getting bigger! The later 1000 cc capacity GS trail bike that usually stays on road rather than off

Left and above

Reverse development meant the original GS trail bike eventually also begat the 'monoshock' R80 and R100RT series Tourers

Overleaf

Martin Wimmer on the Krauser four valve head BMW leading Dennis Noyce's Ducati during Daytona's Battle of the Twins Race in 1984

Below
A cantilever rear-ended private development 1000 cc Boxer BMW being raced during 1985 at the Le Mans 24 hours

Right
Racing Boxers still going strong, Bert Stuckert and Ward Rodgery, Daytona 1987

Opposite
Former TT winner Hans Otto Butenuth seen here on his BMW at Quarter Bridge during the 1989 Senior Race

1992's latest Retro style Boxer, the R100R

All mod cons on this R100, and judging by the bike's general condition, we do think the passenger might need them!

How long can the traditional Boxer engine design live on? Who knows but a while yet if BMW's Projectol is anything to go by

An entirely new model

A slump in the sales of the traditional 'boxer' BMW twins in the late 1970s concentrated the minds of the German factory. Things were so serious that a new management team took over on 1 January 1979 and just seven weeks later the small staff working under Josef Fritzenwenger on the K model was expanded to 240. By this time the basic layout of the new generation BMW had been decided on – it was to be a water-cooled, double overhead-camshaft in-line four-cylinder with the crankshaft in-line with the wheels.

This was to drive the rear wheel via the traditional BMW car type clutch and five-speed gearbox with shaft drive. Although a complete break with the across-the-frame layout of previous multi-cylinder engines, this concept offered a number of advantages. First, it was unique as far as production motorcycles were concerned which was an important point in an overcrowded market. Second, it made mechanical sense: it afforded a low centre of gravity, it was mechanically accessible with the cylinder head sticking out one side and the crankcase the other and it was ideally suited to shaft drive.

The layout was patented as the 'Compact Drive System' (CDS) and the design team got down to work to iron out the many problems and finalize the design which had to be practical and with built-in longevity rather than obsolescence. In other words the K was to carry on the BMW tradition of sound engineering allied to performance and long life.

Four years later, in October 1983, the K100 was introduced to the world press at a launch in the South of France. It made an immediate impression. The in-line engine had a bore and stroke of 67 × 70 mm to give an exact capactiy of 987 cc and produced 90 bhp at 8000 rpm which was enough to give this unstreamlined model an acceleration figure of 0–60 mph in 4.3 sec. and a top speed of around the 125 mph mark.

On the road the delightfully smooth four-cylinder engine was a revelation. Designed by a team led by Martin Probst, who had played a big part in the development of BMW's winning Formula Two racing car power unit, it produced effortless acceleration and power. The only criticism was that the machine felt undergeared and therefore slightly 'fussy' compared to the long-legged gait of the big twin BMWs.

But there was no denying that the BMW design team had achieved their objective of producing an entirely new, fast, flexible and torquey, quality motorcycle. Before the end of 1983 the second model was on sale – the K100RS sports version with streamlining and a claimed top speed of 133 mph. This was quickly followed in the spring of 1984 by the K100RT – the luxury touring variant with a more leisurely riding position and comprehensive fairing.

Left
The original style, fuel injected flat four cylinder K100 of 1983

Overleaf
The fully faired KRS arrived during 1984

All three used the same engine and rolling chassis with telescopic forks, swinging single-sided rear suspension and Italian Brembo disc brakes fore and aft. Only the streamlining and riding positions were different. The three machines proved an incredible sales success. For perhaps the first time the BMW pricing was competitive and despite a difficult market no less than 46,568 K models were sold during the first two years of production – an all-time record for BMW motorcycles.

There had long been rumours of a three-cylinder variant. In fact a very early sneak photograph of a factory tester on a K prototype clearly showed a three-cylinder engine but the press had to wait until September 1985 before the K75 was unveiled at an Austrian reception. Obviously there were technical problems, not least of which was the balance factor of a three-cylinder unit, to be overcome, but to all intents and purposes the new engine was three-quarters of the original K100.

The bore and stroke remained the same to give 740 cc and the engine produced 75 bhp at 8500 rpm. The problem of balance was solved by the addition of a balance shaft within the crankcase and some claim that this made the new engine even smoother than the four – certainly there was little in it. The model at the launch was the K75C tourer. This was quickly followed (in June 1986) by the K75S sporty model with modified suspension and at the Cologne Show towards the end of the year by two further triples – the K75 and the limited edition K75SS. The former a 'budget' version and the latter aimed at the enthusiast who will pay a lot extra for a more exclusive model – in this case the K75S plus fairing around the engine and a more distinctive paint job.

At the same time the four-cylinder K100 series was further expanded by the addition of the K100LT. This was a 'super tourer' aimed mainly at the American market. The specification included not only high quality panniers and a neat top box with built-in back rest for the passenger but also a radio-cassette with twin speakers.

A major technical 'first' was achieved in 1987 when the K100 was offered with an anti-lock ABS braking system – a big step forward for the motorcycling world for no other vehicle is so vunerable as the two-wheeler to a skid induced by a locked wheel.

While all this K series activity was going on the traditional flat-twins were still being produced and 'new' models, with fairly minor changes, introduced. In 1984 the R80 range of three models was up-dated with a new rear swing arm, a new front fork and with wheels similar to those fitted to the K series.

Phil Lovett raced a 'straight from the crate' KRS in the 1985 Production TT

Previous page, above and right
The three cylinder 750 cc came along during 1985, and is now preferred by many to the 1000s or 1100s

The sluggish R45 and the R65 and R100 models were phased out though BMW did continue to produce an 'insurance special' for the home market – a 27 bhp version of the re-vamped R80 engine. This had smaller valves and breathed through smaller carburettors.

Originally the intention was to scrap the larger 980 cc twins but it was such a simple matter to build the R80 engine as a 980 cc that the marketing division could not resist the temptation to launch a 'limited edition' of machines powered by the bigger engines. The first to appear was the re-born sports R100RS in 1986 followed by the touring R100RT a year later and the magnificently brutish R100GS in 1988. Like the R80GS this was an out-and-out sports machine with enduro potential modelled on the Paris-Dakar winning machines. The chassis, with long-travel Italian Marzocchi forks, re-designed 'Paralever' rear swing arm and topped by a near 7-gallon capacity fuel tank, was completely new, and, allied to the torquey 60 bhp flat-twin, gave the newcomer outstanding performance. It soon became a best-seller and 10,000 were sold during the first two years of production.

The success of the new K models, supplemented by surprisingly good sales of the twins, prompted the BMW management to give their styling department a free hand to create something rather special. For while the latest machines from Spandau were technically advanced their styling was modern and pleasing rather than trend-setting. That was corrected when the futuristic K1 was unveiled to the public at the 1988 Cologne Show. For here was a machine that captured attention.

Basically it was the K model with the engine modified and up-rated to 100 bhp. There were now four valves per cylinder and the unit was designed to give a wide spread of power. This was slotted into a modified frame with the Paralever rear swing arm and the whole machine was clothed in the most comprehensive streamlining yet seen on a roadgoing motorcycle. And to cap it all this was finished in a variety of garish colour schemes – scarlet red with yellow wheels and graphics of navy blue and yellow. Nothing could have been more different from the old subdued BMW black and white finish.

At first enthusiasts thought the K1 was just a show surprise, like the turbocharged fully-faired flat-twin Futuro exhibited by BMW in 1980. But they were wrong. The K1, which because of the excellent streamlining is capable of close to 150 mph on the autobahn, went on sale in 1989 and looks set to carry the blue and white quartered BMW badge into the 21st century.

Above
Journalist Mac McDiamid racing his standard KRS 1000 in the 1986 Production 'A' class TT Race

Right
A KRS 1000 in BMW Motorsport white

Previous page

*Anti-lock brakes (ABS) are fitted to this
1992 KRS model*

Above

*BMW–KRS. Surely one of THE best all-
weather bikes*

A KLT Tourer similarly with ABS

Quite a shock to the system was the brightly coloured, 16 valve K1 on its original launch, though it has been toned down a little since

The original K1 could not be equipped
with panniers, or at least not officially, but
this bike's owner has found a way

Above
Derived from the K1, the ABS equipped
16 valve KRS

Left
The alternative K1 colour scheme for
1991–2

The 1992 Hossack–Wüdo K series BMW showing its highly unusual, near constant steering trail front forks

BMW flat four powered Munch two-wheel (with outriggers) saloon!

Previous page

*What some people will do! A highly
customised 'Brick'*

Above

*The new and even more powerful 1100 cc
KLT Tourer as introduced for 1992*